Loving Hands for Jesus

by Edith Padfield Galambos

Illustrated by
Patricia Mattozzi

CONCORDIA

Publishing House
St. Louis

Dedicated
with much love
to
my grandson, Andrew Michael.
May you always have
loving hands
for
Jesus.

Copyright © 1985 Concordia Publishing House
3558 S. Jefferson Avenue, St. Louis, MO 63118-3968
Manufactured in the United States of America

Library of Congress Cataloging in Publication Data

Galambos, Edith Padfield, 1932-
    Loving hands for Jesus.

    (God's little learner series)
    Summary: Describes how our hands can be used to serve Jesus and to show love.
    1. Hand—Religious aspects—Christianity—Juvenile literature. 2. Service (Theology)—
Juvenile literature. 3. Jesus Christ—Juvenile literature. |1. Hand—Religious aspects.
2. Christian life| I. Title. II. Series.
BT738.4.G35   1985   248.8'2   85-7793
ISBN 0-570-08951-4

1 2 3 4 5 6 7 8 9 10   DP   94 93 92 91 90 89 88 87 86 85

My hands are very useful,
They can be helpful, too.
    In work and in play
    All through each day
They do what I tell them to do.

Jesus helps them to be loving;
I ask Him when I pray.
    Like Jesus above
    My hands can show love
Today and every day.

Hands are a special gift from God.
They can be used to do many things.
With four fingers on top
   and a thumb on the side,
each hand is exactly the right shape
   for working and playing,

   for helping and praying.
No one but God could have thought of
   a gift as wonderful as hands.

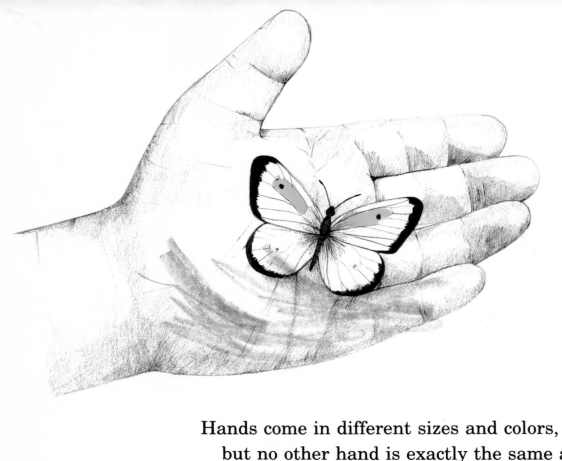

Hands come in different sizes and colors,
    but no other hand is exactly the same as mine.
God was careful to give me the hands just right for me:
    two matching hands,
    ready to do whatever I teach them to do.

God made hands
   for loving
      and touching
         and helping—
just as the hands of Jesus did.

Hands can be very useful.
Hands can show love.

My daddy's hands are strong.
He uses them to do many things.
Strong hands can be working hands.
Strong hands can
    chop wood,
    change a flat tire,
    move heavy furniture.
Strong hands can carry me when I'm tired.

Sometimes, when I am afraid,
Daddy's strong hands hold me tight.
Strong hands can be very useful.
Strong hands can be
    loving hands for Jesus.

My mother's hands are very pretty.
She uses them to do many things.
Pretty hands can be busy hands.
Pretty hands can
    bake bread for our family,
    clean the house,
    play happy songs on the piano.
Pretty hands can take care of me when I'm sick.

Sometimes, when my mother kisses me,
I like to squeeze her hand.
Pretty hands can be very useful.

Pretty hands can be
    loving hands for Jesus.

Baby sister's hands are *so* tiny.
She uses them to do many things.
Tiny hands can be fun hands.
Tiny hands can
   shake a rattle,
   wave bye-bye,
   play pat-a-cake.
Tiny hands can throw a kiss to me.
Sometimes, Baby's hands
hold tightly to my fingers.

Tiny hands can be very useful.
Tiny hands can be
   loving hands for Jesus.

My hands, too, are just right for being
  loving hands for Jesus.
My hands help me work.
They are just the right size
  to hang up my clothes,
  to pick up my toys,
  to carry out the trash.
It is fun to teach my hands to
  do new things.

My hands help me play, too.
They are just the right size
   to catch a ball,
   to color a picture,
   to pet my puppy.
It is fun to trace around my hand on paper.

My hands are just the right size
to show my love for Jesus
    by raking leaves for Daddy,
    by dusting furniture for Mother,
    by rocking Baby to sleep in her cradle,
    by carrying mail to Grandpa,
    by bringing a glass of water to Grandma;
and by folding my hands just so
    to pray to Jesus.

As I grow, my hands will grow with me.
My hands will always be learning to do new things.
Soon they will know how to tie my shoelaces.
My hands do just what I tell them to do.

My hands can be very useful.
My hands can show love.
My hands can be
    loving hands for Jesus.